# A Kid's Guide to Drawing America™

# How to Draw Ohio's Sights and Symbols

Aileen Weintraub

The Rosen Publishing Group's
PowerKids Press™
New York

First Edition

Editors: Jennifer Landau, Jennifer Way
Book Design: Kim Sonsky
Layout Design: Nick Sciacca

Illustration Credits: Emily Muschinske
Photo Credits: p. 7 © Bettmann/CORBIS; p. 8 © Monroe County Historical Commission Archives; p. 9 © Cincinnati Museum Center Image Archives; pp. 12, 14 © One Mile Up, Incorporated; p. 16 © www.corbis.com/CORBIS; p. 18 © Philip Perry; Frank Lane Picture Agency/CORBIS; p. 20 © Richard Hamilton Smith/CORBIS; p. 22 © Ralph A. Clevenger/CORBIS; p. 24 (exterior) © Bill Ross/CORBIS, (guitar) © Conrad Zobel/CORBIS; p. 26 (astronauts) © CORBIS, (*Apollo 11*) © Photri-Microstock; p. 28 © Lee Snider; Lee Snider/CORBIS.

Weintraub, Aileen, 1973–
        How to draw Ohio's sights and symbols / Aileen Weintraub.
            p. cm. – (A kid's guide to drawing America)
        Includes index.
        Summary:  This book explains how to draw some of Ohio's sights and symbols, including the state seal, the official flower, and the cardinal, Ohio's state bird.
        ISBN 0-8239-6091-9
        1. Emblems, State—Ohio—Juvenile literature  2. Ohio—
In art—Juvenile literature    3. Drawing—Technique—Juvenile literature
[1. Emblems, State—Ohio    2. Ohio    3. Drawing—Technique]
I. Title    II. Series
        2002
        743'.8'99771–dc21

Manufactured in the United States of America

# CONTENTS

# Let's Draw Ohio

More than 10,000 years ago, Native Americans populated the land that is now Ohio. In 1669, Frenchman René-Robert Cavelier de La Salle explored the land for France. England took control of the land after the French and Indian War, a land war between France and England that lasted from 1754 to 1763. In 1787, Ohio became part of the Northwest Territory. This was a large, unsettled territory owned by the United States. On March 1, 1803, Ohio became the seventeenth state in the Union. The name Ohio comes from the Iroquois language and means "great river."

Today more than half of Ohio is made up of farmland. Ohio's agriculture includes soybeans, corn, oats, dairy products, and cattle. The state is also an industrial leader. The city of Akron is known for producing rubber. Cincinnati produces jet engines and machine tools, and Toledo produces glass and car parts. Coal is Ohio's biggest natural resource.

Ohio is considered part of America's heartland because it is near the middle of the United States. Ohio has many interesting sites, including more than 10,000 ancient Native American burial mounds. There are many museums and attractions in Ohio, too. These include the Rock and Roll Hall of Fame and the Pro Football Hall of Fame.

This book will teach you about the sights and symbols of the great state of Ohio and how to draw them. Each drawing starts with a simple step. New steps are added in red until the drawing is complete. To shade parts of your drawings, tilt your pencil and rub it back and forth on the paper.

You will need the following supplies to draw Ohio's sights and symbols:

- A sketch pad
- An eraser

- A number 2 pencil
- A pencil sharpener

These are some of the shapes and drawing terms you need to know to draw Ohio's sights and symbols:

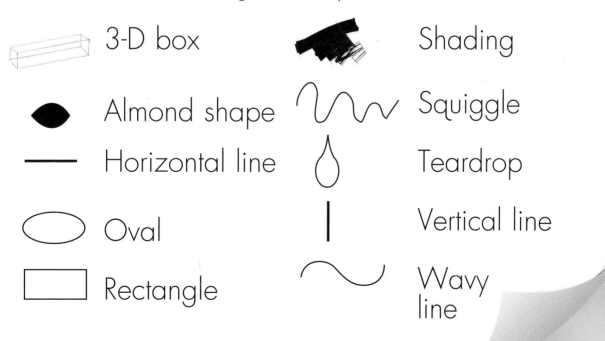

3-D box

Shading

Almond shape

Squiggle

Horizontal line

Teardrop

Oval

Vertical line

Rectangle

Wavy line

# The Buckeye State

Ohio is a place of many firsts. It was the first place to have either an ambulance service or police cars. It is the home of the first professional baseball team, the Cincinnati Reds. A lot of very important people come from Ohio, including seven U.S. presidents. Thomas Edison, the inventor, and the Wright brothers, the inventors of the first self-propelled airplane, came from Ohio. Famous astronauts Neil Armstrong and John Glenn also came from this state. Director Steven Spielberg, poet Rita Dove, and actor Paul Newman are all from Ohio.

The capital of Ohio is Columbus, which is also the state's most populated city. Ohio got the nickname the Buckeye State because of the buckeye trees that once grew on the hills and the plains. There is another reason for the nickname. When William Henry Harrison ran for president in 1840, he made the buckeye tree the symbol of his campaign. He won the race and became the ninth president of the United States.

When William Henry Harrison (1773–1841) ran for president, his opponent, President Martin Van Buren, called him the "log cabin candidate." Van Buren meant that he did not think Harrison was fit to be president, because he enjoyed living in a simple log cabin. Harrison won the election, but he died in office that same year.

# Artist in Ohio

Robert Scott Duncanson

Robert Scott Duncanson was one of the first African American painters to earn a living solely from his art. He was also one of the first African American painters known not only throughout the United States but also in Europe. Duncanson was part of the Hudson River school. Artists of the Hudson River school focused on creating soft, romantic scenes from nature. Duncanson painted many different subjects, but he was best known for his landscapes.

There are no clear records of Duncanson's birth date. It is believed that he was born between 1817 and 1823, in upstate New York. His mother was a free African American woman during the time of slavery. His father was a white man from Canada. Duncanson went to public school in Canada. His parents eventually moved to Cincinnati, Ohio. An antislavery group raised money to send Duncanson to Glasgow, Scotland, to study art. When he returned to Cincinnati in 1842, many of his paintings were exhibited in museums. Duncanson died on December 21, 1872.

Duncanson's 1848 painting, *Cincinnati From Covington, Kentucky*, is an example of the soft, peaceful landscapes of the Hudson River school. This oil-on-canvas work measures 25" x 36" (63.5 cm x 91 cm).

# Map of Ohio

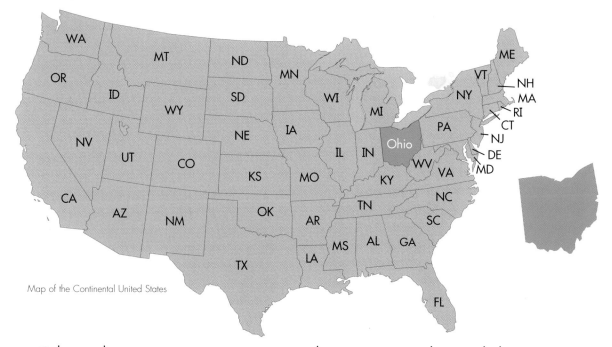

Map of the Continental United States

Ohio has a temperate climate with cold winters and warm summers. It is part of the tornado belt, an area in the Midwest that tornadoes sweep through every spring and fall. This state lies between two bodies of water, Lake Erie to the north and the Ohio River to the south. The states that border Ohio are Indiana, Kentucky, Michigan, Pennsylvania, and West Virginia. Ohio is the thirty-fifth largest state in the country and has a total area of 41,004 square miles (106,200 sq km). The highest point is Campbell Hill at 1,550 feet (472 m) high.

**1**

To begin drawing a map of Ohio, break down the state into basic shapes. Draw a square and a triangle.

**2**

Carefully add the wavy line that makes the southern and the eastern borders of Ohio. This wavy border is formed by the Ohio River.

**3**

Add the crooked border along the top of the state. The most crooked part is formed by Lake Erie. Notice the small islands that are in the lake, and add those to your drawing.

| | |
|---|---|
| ∫ | Ohio River |
| ☆ | Columbus |
| ◉ | Cleveland |
| 🌲 | Wayne National Forest |
| ∿ | Campbell Hill |

**4**

Erase extra lines. Draw a star for the state capital, Columbus. Add a circle for the city of Cleveland, a tree for the Wayne National Forest, and a curved line for Campbell Hill. Finally draw a line along the southern border for the Ohio River.

# The State Seal

Ohio was the first area of land in the Northwest Territory to become a state. The original state seal was created in 1803. Since then it has gone through many changes. The state seal used today was designed in 1967, and it was changed again slightly in 1996. The image of wheat on the seal stands for Ohio's strength in agriculture. The 17 arrows bundled together and the 17 rays shining from the rising sun in the background represent Ohio's status as the seventeenth state. The words "The Great Seal of the State of Ohio" appear around the seal.

1

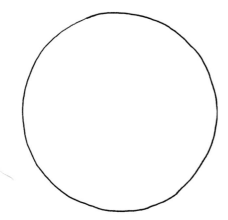

To draw the Ohio state seal, draw a circle.

2

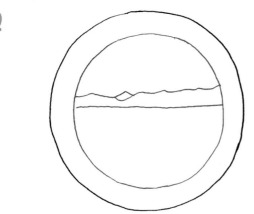

Draw another circle inside the first one. Make a slightly wavy line through the middle of the inner circle for the field. Above that add wavier lines for the mountains.

3

Make a half circle for the sun. Add 17 lines for the sun's rays.

4

Draw a dark, shaded area that stretches diagonally across the circle. This is a place where the field has been plowed.

5

Draw two bundles in the front, or the foreground. Draw 17 arrows in the bundle on the left. Draw wheat in the bundle on the right.

6

Add shading to the mountains. Write the words "THE GREAT SEAL OF THE STATE OF OHIO" between the inner and the outer circles, and you are done.

# The State Flag

Ohio's state flag is the only state flag that looks like a bird's tail. Every other state flag is rectangular. Cleveland-born architect John Eisemann designed this flag. It was adopted by the state on May 9, 1902.

The large, blue triangle represents Ohio's hills and valleys. The red and white stripes on the flag stand for Ohio's roads and waterways. The 13 stars nearest the circle stand for the original 13 colonies. The four stars at the right in the triangle were added to make 17 stars altogether. This is because Ohio is the seventeenth state. The white O in the center stands for Ohio. The red center of the O stands for the state's nickname, the Buckeye State, because the shape looks like the seed of the buckeye tree.

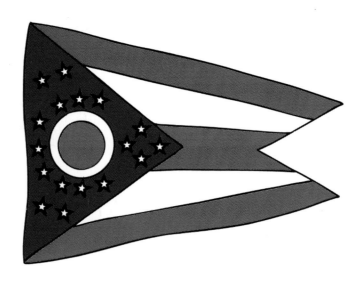

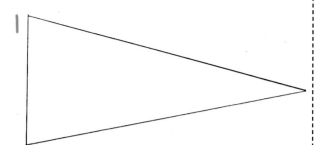

1

To draw Ohio's flag, begin by drawing a triangle on its side.

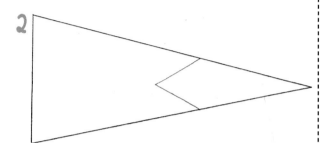

2

Draw a V on its side, inside the triangle.

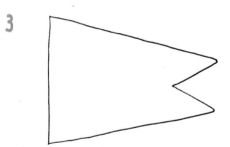

3

Erase extra lines. Now you have the bird's-tail shape of the flag.

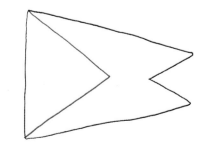

4

Draw a triangle inside the flag.

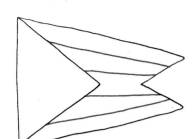

5

Add four lines. These will be colored in later and will become the flag's red and white stripes.

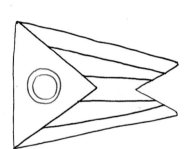

6

Add an O to the center of the inner triangle.

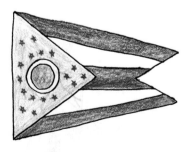

7

Draw 17 small stars around the O. Shade your drawing, and you are done.

# The Scarlet Carnation

The scarlet carnation (*Dianthus caryophyllos*) was chosen as Ohio's state flower in 1904. It was chosen in memory of President William McKinley, who always wore a red carnation on his lapel. McKinley was born in Niles, Ohio, on January 29, 1843. He was elected the twenty-fifth president of the United States on November 3, 1896. One day when he was greeting people, he greeted a young girl who asked him if he could give her something by which to remember their meeting. McKinley gave her his red carnation. The next person to greet the president assassinated him. After the president's death, McKinley supporters decided to make the carnation the state flower. Carnations are now grown in greenhouses in Alliance, Ohio. This city is often called Carnation City.

**1**

Begin with an upside-down triangle. The bottom should be flat, and the top should be slightly curved.

**2**

Add the slanted, rectangular shape of the stem.

**3**

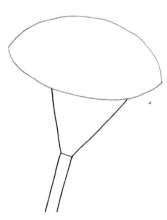

Look at the basic shape of the flower. It looks like an almond. Draw that shape to use as your guide.

**4**

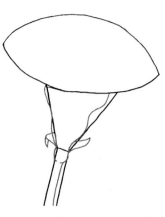

Look at the shape of the stem and the base of the flower. Redraw the curved lines over your guides. Add the two tiny leaves on each side of the stem.

**5**

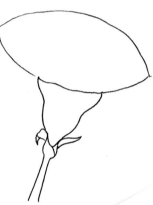

Erase extra lines.

**6**

Begin working on the flower. The carnation has many petals that are very close together. They have crooked edges. Hold your pencil loosely and let your hand draw a lot of layers of wiggly lines inside the oval guide. Erase your guideline and shade.

# The Buckeye Tree

The buckeye tree (*Aesculus glabra*) has a light, soft wood that early pioneers used to make furniture. It became Ohio's state tree in 1953. This tree is small to medium in size and has broad, flat leaves. It grows along the banks, the streams, and the rivers of Ohio. Native Americans called the fruit of the tree *hectuck*. This means "eye of buck." A buck is a male animal, usually a deer or an antelope. They chose this name for the fruit because it looks like a buck's eye. The fruit is round, brown, and glossy. Although the fruit is thought to be poisonous to humans, some people believe that if you carry a buckeye seed in your pocket, you are sure to have good luck.

**1**

Begin with curved lines for the trunk.
Notice that the trunk splits into two thick,
*V*-shaped branches.

**2**

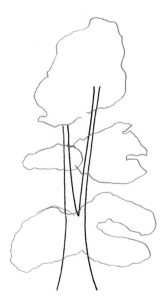

Outline the fluffy, leafy areas using several
round, lumpy shapes.

**3**

Carefully fill in the look of the bark. Buckeye
trees have a unique pattern in the bark.
Shade the bark after you draw this pattern.

**4**

Fill in the leafy area. Use your pencil to
create the look of the leaves. Make many
dark, squiggly lines. Notice that some leafy
areas are darker than others.

# The Cardinal

The cardinal (*Cardinalis cardinalis*) became Ohio's state bird in 1933. Cardinals' beautiful songs can be heard all around Ohio, but the birds prefer to live in deep forests and swamps. They can also be found in fields, orchards, and gardens. These red-feathered birds nest in bushes and trees. They collect dried leaves and grass to make their homes. A female cardinal lays up to six eggs at a time. When the young leave the nest, they follow their parents around for a few days. Then the young birds leave to look for food on their own. Cardinals' favorite meals include fruit, seeds, grass, and insects.

1

Draw an oval for the cardinal's body.

2

Add a triangle to the top. Notice its curve.

3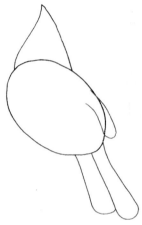

Draw two long, rounded tail feathers and a rounded wing feather.

4

Draw a beak using two sideways triangles on top of each other. The cardinal's beak is short, wide, and curved where the two triangles meet.

5

Add the outline of the cardinal's black mask. Add the eyes.

6

Draw a branch and feet. Add detail to the cardinal's head. Erase extra lines.

7

Add detail and shading. Great job!

21

# The Ladybug

In 1975, a group of schoolchildren from Toledo, Ohio, voted the ladybug (*Coccinellidae sp.*) the official state insect. This vote, however, has never been passed into law. The full name of the ladybug is the ladybird beetle. The ladybug is a beetle that is red or orange with black dots. A female ladybug can lay from 200 to 500 orange-colored eggs at a time. Larvae develop from these eggs. The larvae look like tiny, fat alligators. Soon these little "alligators" turn into ladybugs. These insects live in fields, forests, and gardens. Farmers like to keep ladybugs around, because they eat other insects. This helps to keep the farmers' crops safe.

1

The ladybug can be drawn using very simple shapes. Begin by drawing two ladybug wings by making two flattened oval shapes.

2

Next draw a smaller, flattened oval for the ladybug's middle.

3

Add a smaller oval for the head.

4

Add the antennae and the ladybug's spots. You can draw the pattern you see here or you can make up your own pattern. The two sides should mirror each other.

5

Draw the ladybug's six dark legs.

6

Add shading and detail. Wonderful work!

# The Rock and Roll Hall of Fame

The Rock and Roll Hall of Fame is on the shore of Lake Erie in Cleveland. This building is dedicated to the hundreds of  musicians, songwriters, performers, and producers who have shaped the history of rock-and-roll music. The seven-story building opened its doors in 1995. It is filled with exhibits, films, and videos about rock history. The building itself has a very unique design. I. M. Pei was the architect who designed this building. He was born in China in 1917 and has designed more than 50 projects in the United States, including the John F. Kennedy Library near Boston and the Jacob K. Javits Center in New York City.

1

Let's draw an electric guitar to represent the Rock and Roll Hall of Fame. Begin with a wide circle with an oval on top of it.

2

Outline the shape of the guitar's body.

3

Erase extra guidelines.

4

Add a rectanglar shape for the guitar's neck and a square in the center of the guitar's body.

5

Add a curved shape to the top of the guitar. This is where you tune the guitar's strings.

6

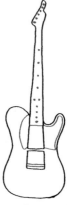

Add the dots along the neck and the tuning screws on the top of the guitar. Add the outline of the dark panel on the guitar's body.

7

Add shading and detail.

25

# The Neil Armstrong Air & Space Museum

The Neil Armstrong Air & Space Museum in Wapakoneta, Ohio, is named for the first man to walk on the Moon. The museum opened in 1972. It is filled with interactive exhibits and with many artifacts from the *Apollo 11* space mission, including a rock from the Moon. Ohio-born Neil Armstrong was one of the astronauts on *Apollo 11*, the first manned spacecraft to land on the Moon. It

touched down on the Moon's surface on July 20, 1969. This mission paved the way for future space exploration. This exciting museum even has the Astro-theater, a theater that allows visitors to experience the sights and the sounds of space exploration.

**1**

Let's draw *Apollo 11* to represent the Neil Armstrong Air & Space Museum. Begin with a long rectangle shape. Add a cone to the top. Add a rounded tip to the cone. The cone and the rounded tip make up the capsule. This is where Neil Armstrong rode.

**2**

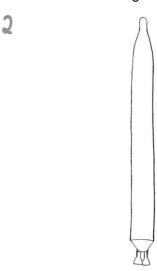

Erase extra lines. Add a triangular bottom with two conelike shapes below it.

**3**

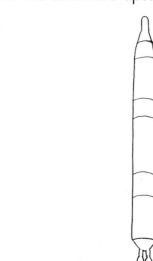

Draw *Apollo 11*'s sections using curved lines.

**4**

Decorate *Apollo 11* with patterns and shades of gray. Pay attention to these patterns.

**5**

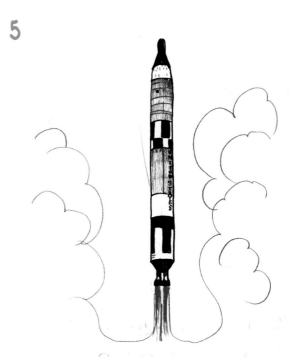

Add details to the ship. Draw smoke and flames coming out of the bottom, and you're done.

# Ohio's Capitol

When Ohio first became a state in 1803, the capital city was Chillicothe. In 1816, Columbus, Ohio, became the state's permanent capital city. The capitol building is located in Capitol Square on 10 acres (4 ha) of land. The building was constructed in 1861. In 1996, the grounds underwent a major restoration. The building is considered Greek Revival architecture, which means that it looks like a building from ancient Greece. Capitol Square has a veterans memorial that honors all the Ohioans who have served in the U.S. military. There are also fountains, statues, and even sculptures on the grounds. The capitol building is one of the oldest state houses still in use today.

**1**

Begin with a slanted rectangle. Notice that in the photo, the building gets smaller and narrower as it gets farther away from you. The slanted rectangle should get narrower, too. Add the ledge to the top of the rectangle. The ledge should get narrower as well.

**2**

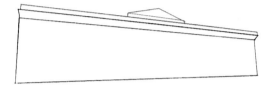

Draw another slanted rectangle for the roof layer. Add a triangle to the roof layer. This is called the pediment.

**3**

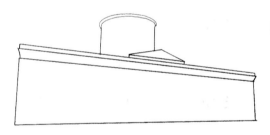

Behind the triangle, draw a cylinder with a curved line at the top to show the rooftop's edge.

**4**

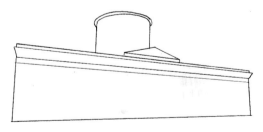

Add another line to the bottom rectangle.

**5**

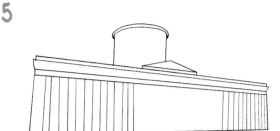

The front of the building has a pattern of dark and light areas. This was done so that the building would not look like one big, heavy block. The dark and light bands make the building look more interesting. Draw several lines across the front of the building. Leave the middle area open.

**6**

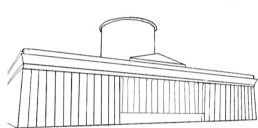

The middle area has columns holding up the roof. The columns are long cylinders. Add lines along the roof line of the left side of the building. Notice how the angle makes the building look three-dimensional.

**7**

Shade the building, notice the dark and light areas. Add windows to the darker areas. Great job!

# Ohio State Facts

| | |
|---|---|
| Statehood | March 1, 1803, 17th state |
| Area | 41,004 square miles (106,200 sq km) |
| Population | 11,256,708 |
| Capital | Columbus, population, 657,100 |
| Most Populated City | Columbus |
| Industries | Rubber, jet engines, machine tools, glass, steel, car parts |
| Agriculture | Soybeans, corn, oats, dairy products, cattle |
| Tree | Buckeye (*Aesculus glabra*) |
| Motto | With God All Things Are Possible |
| Nickname | The Buckeye State |
| Insect | Ladybug (*Coccinellidae sp.*) |
| Bird | Cardinal (*Cardinalis cardinalis*) |
| Flower | Scarlet carnation (*Dianthus caryophyllos*) |
| Gemstone | Flint |
| Song | "Beautiful Ohio" |

# Glossary

**ancient** (AYN-chent)  Very old, from a long time ago.

**artifacts** (AR-tih-fakts)  Objects created and produced by humans.

**assassinated** (uh-SA-sin-ayt-ed)  To have murdered an important or famous person.

**capsule** (KAP-suhl)  A compartment of a spacecraft that carries astronauts or other instruments.

**exhibits** (eg-ZIB-its)  Objects or pictures set out for people to see.

**exploration** (ek-spluh-RAY-shun)  To travel through little-known land.

**industrial** (in-DUS-tree-ul)  Having to do with systems of work, or labor.

**interactive** (in-tuh-RAK-tiv)  Hands-on activities to help show how something works.

**landscapes** (LAND-skayps)  Views of scenery on land.

**lapel** (luh-PEL)  The fold on the front of a coat.

**larvae** (LAR-vee)  The plural form of larva. The early life stage of certain animals that differs greatly from the adult stage.

**opponent** (uh-POH-nent)  A person or a group that is against another in a fight, a contest, or a discussion.

**pediment** (PEH-duh-ment)  A triangular space on the roof of a building that often is decorated with sculptures or carvings.

**pioneers** (py-uh-NEERZ)  Some of the first people to settle in a new area.

**poisonous** (POY-zun-us)  Something that could make you very sick or that could kill you.

**restoration** (reh-stuh-RAY-shun)  Working to fix something to make it look better.

**symbol** (SIM-bul)  An object or a design that stands for something important.

**temperate** (TEM-peh-ret)  Moderate, not extreme.

**territory** (TER-uh-tor-ee)  Land that is controlled by a person or group.

**unique** (yoo-NEEK)  Being one of a kind.

# Index

# Web Sites

To learn more about Ohio, check out these Web sites:
www.ohiotravel.com
www.rockhall.com
www.statehouse.state.oh.us